The Man Who Set the Town Dancing

El hombre que puso a bailar a todo el pueblo

The Man Who Set the Town Dancing

El hombre que puso a bailar a todo el pueblo

Written by / escrito por Candice Stanford
Illustrated by / ilustrado por Flo Hosa Dougherty

Clear Light Publishers
Santa Fe, New Mexico

DEDICATION
To Cassaundra and RachelLauren, my two greatest dreams.

ACKNOWLEDGMENTS

The author and illustrator express their gratitude to our publisher for patience and gracious assistance; as well as to Denise Chavez, review comment; Hermes and Margaret Pedreny and Fernando Mayans, Spanish translations; Gene Zika, music arrangement with added guitar chords; Vladimir Chaloupka, photography; Barbara Alpher, moral support; David Lee Summers, advice and encouragement; State National Bank, promotion.

And to the reality that dreams do come true!

© 2002 by Candice Stanford and Flo Hosa Dougherty
Clear Light Publishers
823 Don Diego, Santa Fe, New Mexico 87505
web site: www.clearlightbooks.com

First Edition
10 9 8 7 6 5 4 3 2 1

Library of Congress Cataloging-in-Publication Data

Stanford, Candice, 1957–
    The man who set the town dancing = El hombre que puso a bailar a todo el pueblo / by Candice Stanford ; illustrated by Flo Hosa Dougherty.
        p. cm.
    Parallel texts in English and Spanish.
    Summary: Profiles José Tena, who dreamed that someday everyone in his town would know the folk dances from when New Mexico was still a Spanish colony, and who made that dream come true through his Ballet Folklórico.
    Contents: A true story told in both English and Spanish -- The real José Tena: read about the man behind the story -- Four Spanish dances: learn the dances from the book: step diagrams & music.
    ISBN 1-57416-050-8
    1. Tena, José--Juvenile literature. 2. Dancers--New Mexico--Biography--Juvenile literature. 3. Folk dancing, Mexican--Juvenile literature. [1. Tena, José 2. Dancers. 3. Mexican Americans--Biography. 4. Folk dancing, Mexican. 5. Ballet Folklórico de Mexico. 6. Spanish language materials--Bilingual.] I. Title: Hombre que puso a bailar a todo el pueblo. II. Dougherty, Flo Hosa, ill. III. Title.
GV1624.N6 S83 2002
792.8'092--dc21

2002067266
CIP

Jacket art by Flo Hosa Dougherty
Cover design by Carol O'Shea and Marcia Keegan
Book design & illustrations by Flo Hosa Dougherty
Typography & production by Carol O'Shea

Printed in Korea.

Table of Contents

José had a dream. In his dream, he saw brightly colored costumes swirling around, and he heard laughter and tapping shoes. Everyone was dancing.

José tuvo un sueño. En su sueño vio trajes de baile tradicionales de brillantes colores que remolineaban por el aire, y sintió risas y zapateos. Todos estaban bailando.

Every night, José would have the same dream. He thought about this dream over and over again.

Cada noche José tenía el mismo sueño. El pensaba en este sueño sin cesar.

7

More than anything José had ever wished for in his whole life, he wanted to make this dream come true. He wanted to teach all the people in his town to dance. Even the littlest children and all the grandmas and grandpas would learn to dance. When it was time for fiesta, everyone would be dancing.

No había ninguna otra cosa que José hubiera deseado más en su vida que hacer su sueño realidad. El quería enseñarle a toda la gente de su pueblo a bailar. Hasta el más pequeñito, y todos los abuelos y las abuelas, aprenderían. Cuando llegaran las fiestas todos se pondrían a bailar.

The dances José wanted to teach are from a long time ago. They are folk-dances from when New Mexico was still a Spanish colony, way before it became a state.

Los bailes que José quería enseñar son bailes de largo tiempo atrás. Bailes folklóricos, de cuando Nuevo México era todavía colonia de España, mucho antes de llegar a convertirse en un nuevo estado de Estados Unidos.

8

José was worried that soon everyone would completely forget about these dances. Almost no one knew how to dance them anymore.

A José le preocupaba que todo el mundo pronto olvidase estos bailes por completo. Ya casi nadie sabía como bailarlos.

When José put on his dancing shoes and performed at community events, people just sat around and watched. No one joined in because no one knew the steps. This made José sad.

Cuando Jose se ponía sus zapatos de baile y presentaba sus números en los actos comunales, la gente sólo se sentaba a verlo. Nadie se atrevía a acompañarlo porque no sabían los pasos. A José esto lo hacía sentirse muy triste.

And the dances were so much fun! They had brought so much joy and color to the people of colonial New Mexico and were part of their Spanish heritage.

¡Y eran tan amenos estos bailes! Habían traído mucha alegría y dado mucho colorido al pueblo del Nuevo Mexico colonial, además de ser parte de su herencia española.

One dance is called *La Indita*. It is like an old-fashioned polka, danced to violin and guitar music. Another traditional dance is *El Vals de los Paño*s. In this dance, one man dances with two women. He holds two handkerchiefs, one in each hand. A woman holds the other end of each handkerchief. *El Vaquero* is like a cowboy dance. Holding hands, the dancers skip forwards, turn under their arms, then skip back. *Las Cuadrillas* is like a square dance, done with polka steps. All of these dances are lively and fun to do.

Uno de los bailes se llama *La indita*. Es muy parecido a una polca antigua, bailada al son de violines y guitarras. Otro baile tradicional es *El vals de los paños*. En este baile un hombre baila con dos mujeres. El tiene dos pañuelos, uno en cada mano, mientras las mujeres toman la otra punta del pañuelo. Otro baile es *El vaquero*. Tomados de la mano, los bailarines dan un salto hacia delante, giran dando una vuelta por debajo de sus brazos y luego dan un salto atrás. *Las cuadrillas* es como una contradanza con los pasos de la polca. Todos estos bailes están llenos de vida y da gusto bailarlos.

José had an idea of
how to get the people
dancing, but he had no
money to get started. No one
would help him with his dream.
No one cared.

Jose tenía una idea de
cómo hacer para que la
gente se interesara en el
baile, pero no tenía dinero
para empezar y nadie que
lo ayudara con su sueño.
A nadie le importaba.

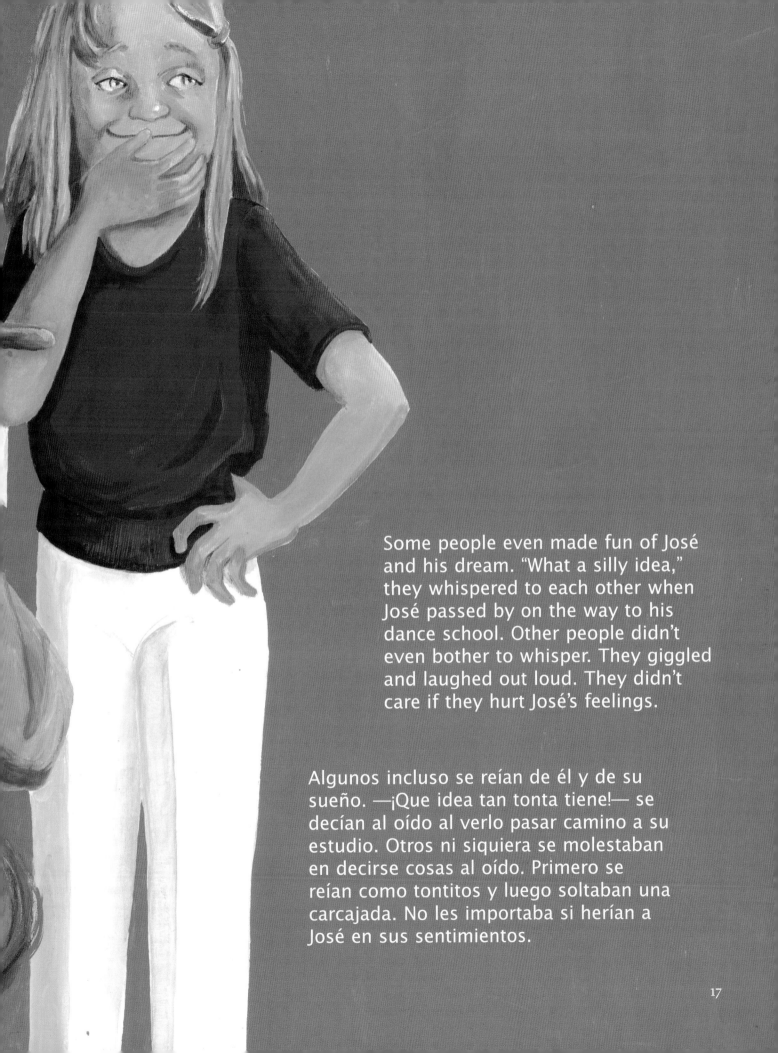

Some people even made fun of José and his dream. "What a silly idea," they whispered to each other when José passed by on the way to his dance school. Other people didn't even bother to whisper. They giggled and laughed out loud. They didn't care if they hurt José's feelings.

Algunos incluso se reían de él y de su sueño. —¡Que idea tan tonta tiene!— se decían al oído al verlo pasar camino a su estudio. Otros ni siquiera se molestaban en decirse cosas al oído. Primero se reían como tontitos y luego soltaban una carcajada. No les importaba si herían a José en sus sentimientos.

But José did not give up. Those people just did not understand. They didn't know the fun they were missing.

Pero José no se dio por vencido. Estas personas simplemente no entendían. Ni sabían de los momentos de alegría que se estaban perdiendo.

José had been dancing for thirty years, since he was a young boy. He danced because the lively steps and rhythms were so much fun. He could not imagine a world without dance. Where would the joy be?

Hacía treinta años que José bailaba, desde que era un jovencito. El bailaba porque los ritmos y los pasos rápidos del baile le gustaban mucho. No podía imaginarse una vida sin baile. ¿En dónde estaría la alegría?

José had also become a ballet folklorico dance teacher and choreographer. Little by little, he started adding the traditional dances of New Mexico to what he was already teaching his classes of children and adults. He taught them *La Indita*, *El Vaquero*, *El Vals de los Paños*, and *Las Cuadrillas*.

Asimismo, José había llegado a ser maestro de danzas folklóricas y coreógrafo. Poco a poco comenzó a enseñar los bailes folklóricos tradicionales de Nuevo México en sus clases para niños y adultos. Les enseñó *La indita*, *El vaquero*, *El vals de los paños* y *Las cuadrillas*.

Wherever José went to teach dance—at the university, an elementary school or a senior citizens center—he always added a few of the folk dances. The people were beginning to see that these dances really were easy and fun. More and more people wanted to learn the dances.

Dondequiera que José iba a enseñar baile, ya fuera en la universidad, en una escuela o en un centro recreativo para jubilados, él siempre incluía algunos bailes folklóricos. La gente empezaba a entender que estos bailes eran realmente sencillos y muy divertidos. Cada vez más gente quería aprenderlos.

24

José taught the folk dances night after night, week after week. A few of his adult students became quite good at the dances, and José asked them if they would be willing to teach others as well. More and more people were able to learn the dances.

José hizo esto noche tras noche, semana tras semana. Algunos de sus estudiantes mayores aprendieron bien los bailes. José les preguntó a ellos, si estaban dispuestos a enseñarles a otros a la vez. Más y más gente pudo entonces aprender los bailes.

Now everyone is dancing. Now the same ones who used to snicker at José reach out to shake his hand—at the post office, or the dentist chair, or on the bike trail— wherever they find him.

Ahora todo el mundo baila. Los mismos que se burlaban de él, ahora le extienden la mano para saludarlo afectuosamente cada vez que lo encuentran en el correo, en el consultorio del dentista o en las rutas para andar en bicicleta; dondequiera que lo encuentren.

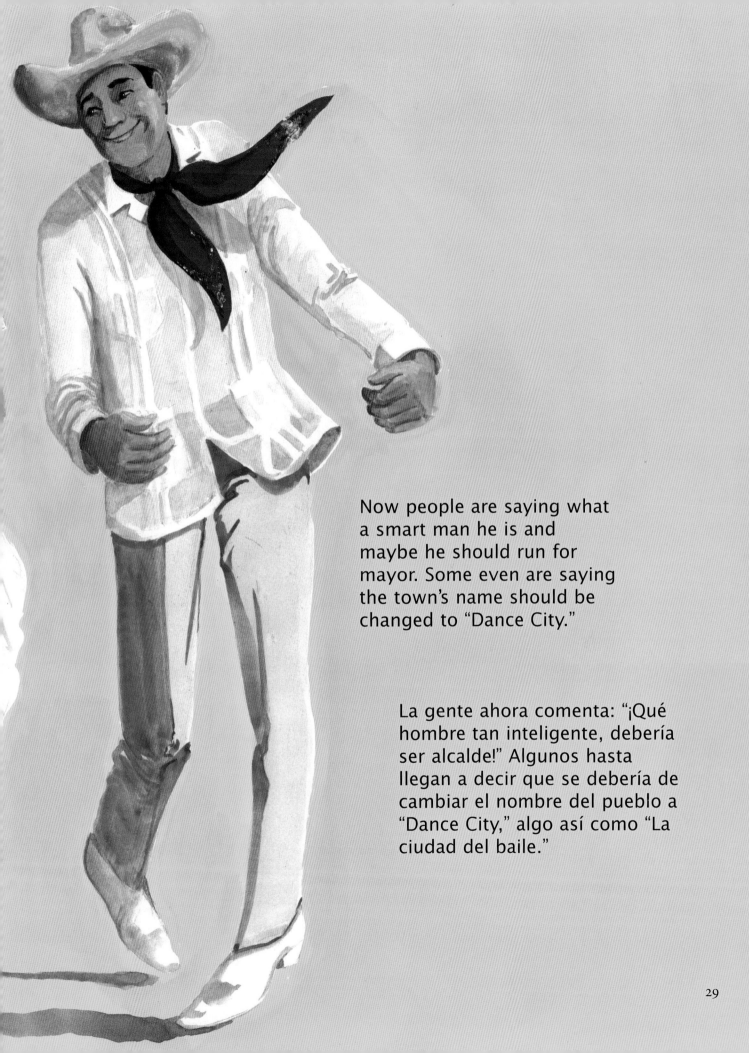

Now people are saying what a smart man he is and maybe he should run for mayor. Some even are saying the town's name should be changed to "Dance City."

La gente ahora comenta: "¡Qué hombre tan inteligente, debería ser alcalde!" Algunos hasta llegan a decir que se debería de cambiar el nombre del pueblo a "Dance City," algo así como "La ciudad del baile."

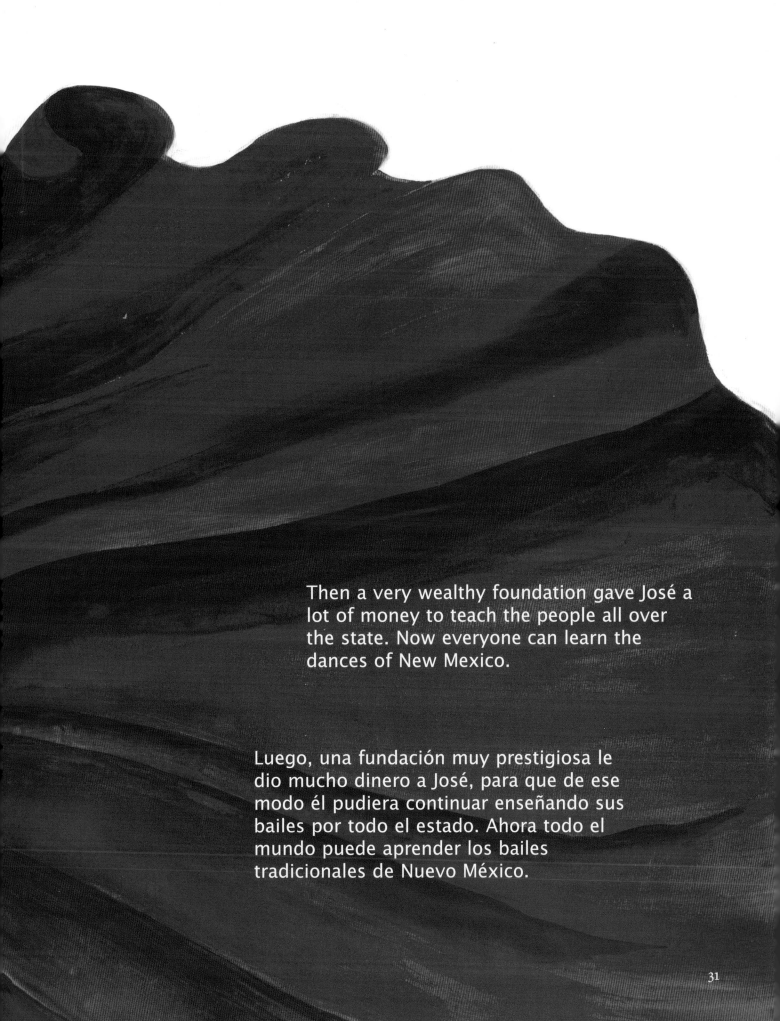

Then a very wealthy foundation gave José a lot of money to teach the people all over the state. Now everyone can learn the dances of New Mexico.

Luego, una fundación muy prestigiosa le dio mucho dinero a José, para que de ese modo él pudiera continuar enseñando sus bailes por todo el estado. Ahora todo el mundo puede aprender los bailes tradicionales de Nuevo México.

31

Today José is still living his dream. Now, when he dances at fiestas and events in the town parks, he no longer dances alone with everyone watching. Now, the people of the town get up out of their seats and dance with him. The people love doing the dances and are so happy that the man who set the town dancing kept going after his dream until it came true.

Aún hoy José vive su sueño. Ahora cuando él baila en las fiestas y en los actos comunales en los parques del pueblo, ya no baila solo, con la gente mirándolo. Ahora la gente se levanta de sus asientos y se pone a bailar con él. A todos les gusta bailar y están muy felices de que "El hombre que puso a bailar a todo el pueblo" haya seguido en busca de su sueño hasta haberlo convertido en realidad.

33

JOSÉ TENA
The Real "Man Who Set the Town Dancing"
El verdadero "hombre que puso a bailar a todo el pueblo"

New Mexico's cultural treasure, José Tena, has been dancing more than three decades on his forever-young legs. He has set thousands more in motion with his dance group of 23 years, known nationally as Ballet Folklorico de la Tierra del Encanto. Some original members still dance with the Ballet.

Tena's personal commitment incorporates a legacy of the past and present by preserving and reviving lively enjoyable folk dances. The diverse culture of Mexico added with the colonial influences of France and Spain offer a rich heritage in grace, style and costume. José combines, refines and choreographs the entire repertoire of his troupe.

The entertaining tradition of the Ballet Folklorico has been enthusiastically received. It has been a mainstay in fiestas, mariachi conferences and special performances. By invitation the Ballet Folklorico has appeared from coast to coast—from the Smithsonian in Washington D.C. to Danzantes Unidos Festival in Fresno, California—and many places in between.

The master of dance, José Tena, is the recipient of several coveted supporting grants for his outstanding contribution to the arts.

Further information about José Tena can be obtained from the Branigan Cultural Center Foundation by addressing your request to 500 N. Water St., Las Cruces, NM 88001.

Phone: (505) 541-2154
Fax: (505) 525-3654
e-mail: josetenadancer@yahoo.com or
joset@las-cruces.org

El maestro José Tena, tesoro cultural de Nuevo México, ha estado en el mundo de la danza por más de tres décadas, enseñando y bailando con inusitado vigor. A través de su grupo, conocido en todo el país como "El Ballet Folklórico de la Tierra del Encanto," el maestro Tena ha sido fuente de inspiración para miles de bailarines por más de 23 años. Algunos de sus primeros miembros todavía permanecen activos.

El cometido personal del maestro Tena consiste en incorporar en el presente, el legado del pasado, preservando y revitalizando las danzas folklóricas más amenas e interesantes. La riqueza cultural de México aunada a las influencias culturales de España y Francia, brindan un rico patrimonio en materia de estilos, trajes de baile tradicionales y donaire. José monta, crea y perfecciona las coreografías de todo el repertorio de su compañía.

El carácter amenizador de El Ballet Folklórico ha tenido una gran aceptación. Siempre ha sido una pieza clave en las fiestas, conferencias de mariachis y representaciones especiales. El Ballet Folklórico ha viajado, por expresa invitación, a lo largo y ancho del país. Innumerables escenarios han acogido sus actuaciones: desde el museo Smithsonian en la ciudad de Washington hasta el Festival de Danzantes Unidos en Fresno, California. El maestro José Tena ha recibido importantes fondos de ayuda de prestigiosas instituciones por su notable contribución a las artes.

Más información sobre el maestro José Tena puede obtenerse a través de la Fundación del Centro Cultural Branigan, ubicada en 500 N. Water St., Las Cruces, New Mexico 88001.

Teléfono: (505) 541-2154
Fax: (505) 525-3654
correo electrónico: josetenadancer@yahoo.com
o joset@las-cruces.org

FOUR NEW MEXICAN FOLK DANCES

Explanation of Diagrams

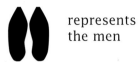 represents the men

 Curved lines are the arms and indicate the direction that each figure is facing.

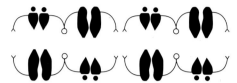

 represents the women

 Couple holding hands and facing in opposite directions

Four couples, holding hands, two sides facing each other. Women on right of men.

It is customary for the men dancers to clap their hands as a signal for the musicians to stop playing after a satisfactory number of repetitions have been made in each dance. Musical instruments used are almost invariably violins and guitars. Couples in square and trio dances designated by A and B.

La Indita (The Little Indian)

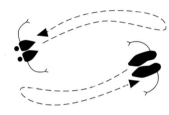

The basic step is similar to the old-fashioned polka. Step right, draw left foot up to right, take a tiny, quick step and hop right with right foot. Repeat left. Danced in regular ballroom position. Dancers stand apart and, each going to right of partner, dance in semi-circle around partner and back. Keep facing all the time.

Music 1. Couples dance in a semicircle. Hold right hands, face same direction. Dance toward nearest couple and back. Dance forward toward nearest couple again and back again.
Music 2. Dancers take regular ballroom position and polka for 16 measures. Repeat all from beginning. The steps are executed in the shuffling manner similar to that of Pueblo Indian dancers.

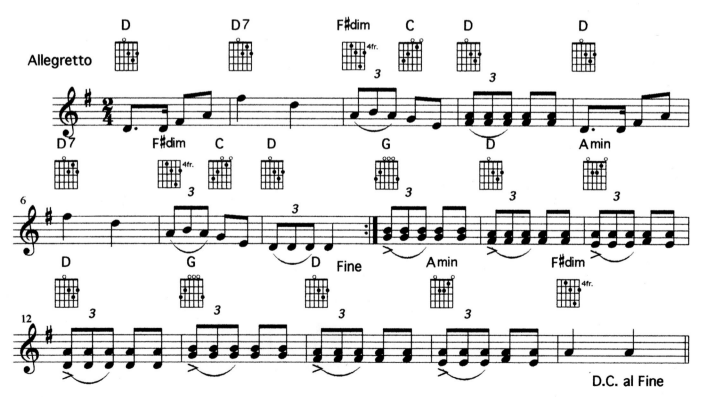

Excerpted from the edited compilation of dances and music by Aurora Lucero-White, Helene Mareau and Eunice Hauskins.

El Vals de los Paños (The Waltz of the Handkerchiefs)

Dancers are arranged in threes, two women for each man (man in center with a woman on each side). Man has two handkerchiefs. He holds one in each hand. Woman on his right takes opposite corner of handkerchief with her left hand. Woman on his left takes opposite corner of handkerchief in her right hand. Trios face each other. The waltz step is used throughout. Dancers must not let go of handkerchiefs at any time during the dance.

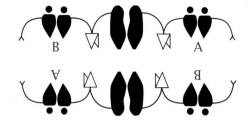

Music 1. Trios waltz forward to center 4 measures. Back 4 measures. Repeat.

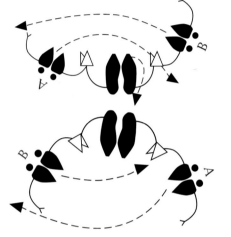

Music 2. Dancers hold arms high. Woman A on man's left dances around man, going under arch formed by arms of man and woman B on his right, while woman B dances around him toward the left, thus making a half circle. Man turns right.

Man makes half turn as women progress around to complete their circles. This time woman B goes under arms of man and woman A. They return to the starting position for Music 1 and repeat all.

Although only one trio is shown in these diagrams, both trios dance the same pattern.

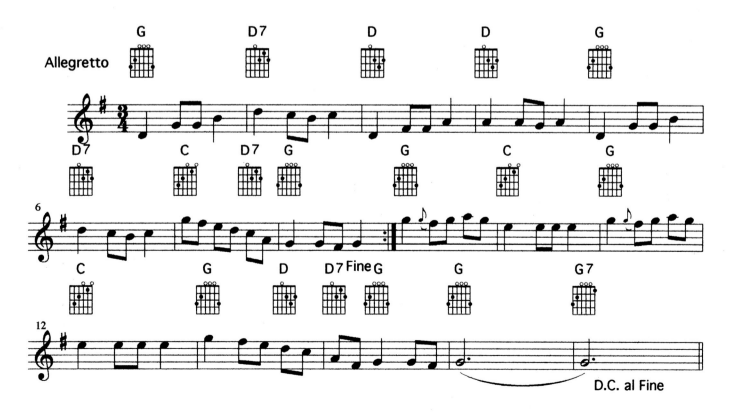

El Vaquero (The Cowboy)

The basic step is a form of skipping. Dancers both face the same direction, holding hands (not crossed). Man takes woman's right hand in his left and her left hand in his right. Starting with right foot up, hop on left foot, take small step forward with right foot, draw left foot up to right, hop on right with left foot raised in front. Repeat.

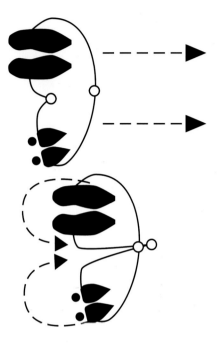

To Music 1. Skipping step described above. Partners holding hands, skip forward.

To Music 2. Still skipping, dancers turn under arms. Turning outwards, arms going over their heads, they keep hold of hands.
   Repeat.
   Return to first step and repeat all.
   The steps of this dance mimic the rollicking liveliness that American cowboys always inject into their dances.

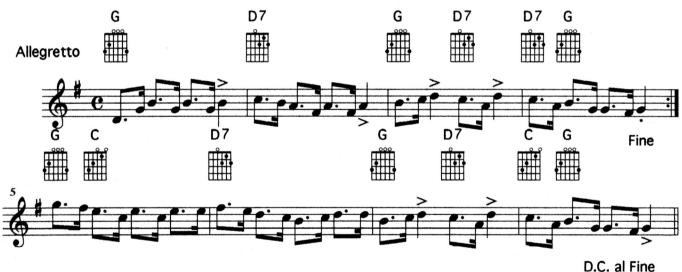

38

Las Cuadrillas (Cuadrilla – Part One)

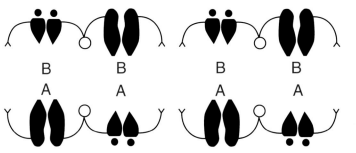

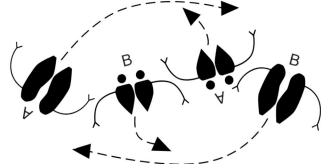

Basic step, polka. Couples stand in square, the two sides facing each other, women on men's right. Couples hold hands.

Music 1. Couples walk forward. Each couple has hands clasped.

Couples let go hands to pass, clasping hands again as soon as passed.

Only right side of square is shown here. Left side dances exactly the same pattern.

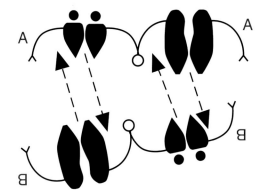

Couples turn and face center again, ready to walk back. They pass again as above, and return to starting position.

Repeat all.

Music 2. All polka. Each with own partner.

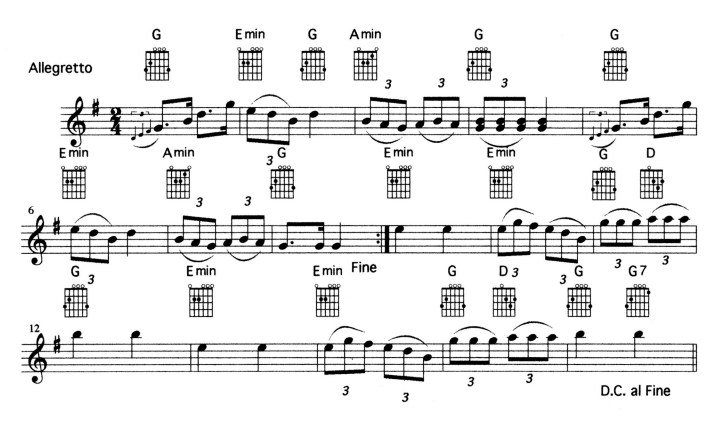

39

ABOUT THE AUTHOR & ILLUSTRATOR

The idea for *The Man Who Set the Town Dancing* came during a newspaper interview Candice Stanford conducted with José Tena, who remarked that his dream was to teach everyone in Las Cruces to dance; hence the "Man Who Set the Town Dancing" was conceived. Tena has been dancing for more than three decades with his dance group, Ballet Folklórico de la Tierra Del Encanto. This group has been a mainstay in local fiestas, mariachi conferences and special performances and has appeared across the country from the Smithsonian in Washington D.C. to the Danzantes Unidos Festival in Fresno, California.

CANDICE STANFORD is a reporter, freelance writer and photographer for newspapers and magazines. Currently a high school journalism and photography teacher in the Seattle area, Stanford formerly wrote a weekly children's book review column for the Las Cruces *Sun News*. She travels extensively, collects children's books and spends her summers teaching in other countries such as Korea. She is looking forward an upcoming assignment in China along with her two daughters. Originally from northern Minnesota, she has a master's degree in curriculum and instruction and is licensed as a K-12 school principal.

FLO HOSA DOUGHERTY is an artist who accepts commissioned requests, exhibits in juried shows and has received numerous awards. She is currently residing in Las Cruces, New Mexico, and visitors are welcome to her home studio/gallery, Blue Gate Gallery. After graduating from Youngstown State University in Ohio, Dougherty served for a number of years as a high school art department chairperson. Encouraging art among young people in her local community is still a priority for her. For more about Flo Hosa Dougherty and to view some of her work, visit her web site at www.artgally.com/bluegate.